EXPLORING SPACE

PROBES

BY DALTON RAINS

WWW.APEXEDITIONS.COM

Copyright © 2024 by Apex Editions, Mendota Heights, MN 55120. All rights reserved. No part of this book may be reproduced or utilized in any form or by any means without written permission from the publisher.

Apex is distributed by North Star Editions:
sales@northstareditions.com | 888-417-0195

Produced for Apex by Red Line Editorial.

Photographs ©: iStockphoto, cover; NASA, 1, 13, 14, 15, 16–17, 18, 19, 20–21 (left), 20–21 (right), 22–23; Shutterstock Images, 4–5, 29; Southwest Research Institute/Johns Hopkins University Applied Physics Laboratory/NASA, 6–7, 8; Roman Tkachenko/Southwest Research Institute/Johns Hopkins University Applied Physics Laboratory/NASA, 9; Bill Ingalls/NASA, 10–11; AP Images, 12; Gerald Eichstädt and Seán Dora/JPL-Caltech/SwRI/MSSS/NASA, 24–25; European Space Agency & NASA/Solar Orbiter/EUI Team/Science Source, 26; Glenn Benson/NASA, 27

Library of Congress Control Number: 2023912748

ISBN
978-1-63738-739-9 (hardcover)
978-1-63738-782-5 (paperback)
978-1-63738-867-9 (ebook pdf)
978-1-63738-825-9 (hosted ebook)

Printed in the United States of America
Mankato, MN
012024

NOTE TO PARENTS AND EDUCATORS

Apex books are designed to build literacy skills in striving readers. Exciting, high-interest content attracts and holds readers' attention. The text is carefully leveled to allow students to achieve success quickly. Additional features, such as bolded glossary words for difficult terms, help build comprehension.

CHAPTER 1
NEW HORIZONS 4

CHAPTER 2
EARLY PROBES 10

CHAPTER 3
GOING FARTHER 16

CHAPTER 4
MORE MISSIONS 22

COMPREHENSION QUESTIONS • 28
GLOSSARY • 30
TO LEARN MORE • 31
ABOUT THE AUTHOR • 31
INDEX • 32

CHAPTER 1

NEW HORIZONS

A small **probe** speeds through space. The spacecraft is called *New Horizons*. It is flying toward Pluto.

Pluto is about 3 billion miles (4.8 billion km) from Earth.

The journey takes several years. Eventually, the probe nears Pluto. It flies past the **dwarf planet**.

LONG TRIP

Pluto is very far away from Earth. *New Horizons* took more than nine years to reach it. The probe passed Jupiter on the way. Jupiter's **gravity** helped the probe gain speed.

New Horizons flew past Pluto on July 14, 2015.

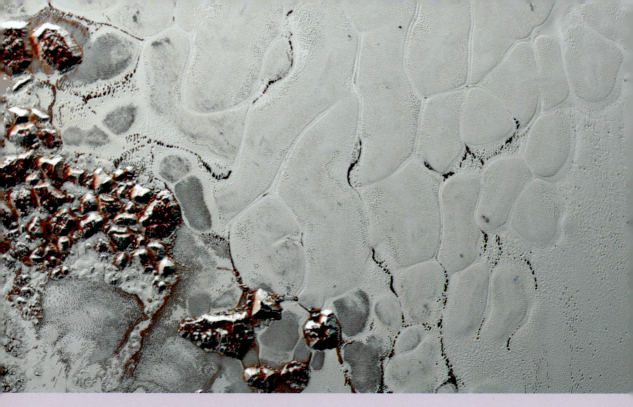

New Horizons took close-up pictures of Pluto's surface.

The probe uses sensors to study Pluto. It also takes many pictures. The probe sends the **data** back to Earth. It helps scientists learn more about the **solar system**.

FAST FACT

New Horizons uses **radio signals**. These signals send data. They take hours to reach Earth.

In 2019, *New Horizons* passed by an object called Arrokoth. It was the farthest object from Earth that a spacecraft had ever passed.

CHAPTER 2

EARLY PROBES

Probes are a type of spacecraft. They fly through space without people. They gather information. They also take measurements.

Scientists can control probes and receive data from Earth.

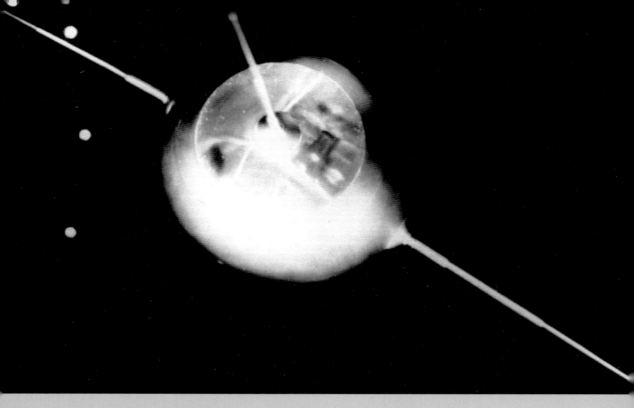

The Soviet Union launched *Sputnik 1* in 1957.

Sputnik 1 was the first probe in space. It **orbited** Earth for three months. Later, the United States launched its first probe.

THE SPACE RACE

The first probe launches began the Space Race. This competition was between the United States and the Soviet Union. They tried to explore parts of space first.

The United States launched its first probe in 1958. It was called *Explorer 1*.

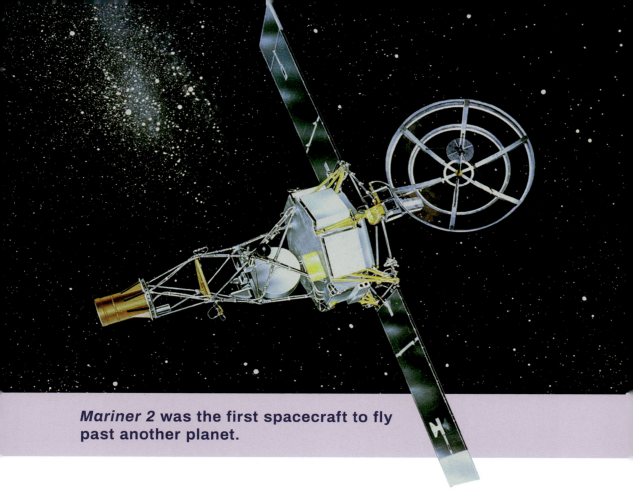

Mariner 2 **was the first spacecraft to fly past another planet.**

Countries sent more probes.

The probes flew past the Moon.

They flew past other planets, too.

Mariner 2 passed Venus in 1962.

FAST FACT
Mariner 4 flew past Mars in 1965. It took pictures of the planet.

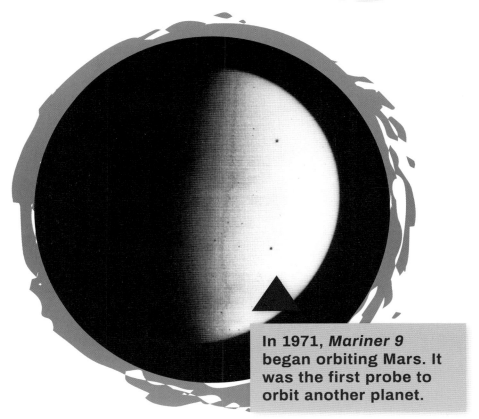

In 1971, *Mariner 9* began orbiting Mars. It was the first probe to orbit another planet.

CHAPTER 3

Going Farther

In the late 1970s, scientists had new goals. They turned to other parts of the solar system. They sent probes to the four outer planets.

The four outer planets of the solar system are Jupiter, Saturn, Uranus, and Neptune.

Voyager 1 took photos of Jupiter's Great Red Spot. This area is an ongoing storm on the planet's surface.

Two probes launched in 1977. They were *Voyager 1* and *Voyager 2*. These probes flew past Jupiter and Saturn.

FAST FACT
The Voyager probes studied Jupiter's moons. They found volcanoes on one.

The Voyager probes passed Saturn in 1980 and 1981. They gathered data about Saturn's atmosphere.

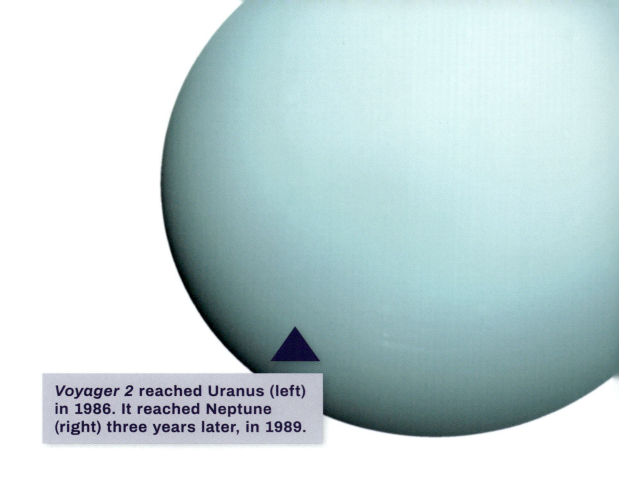

Voyager 2 reached Uranus (left) in 1986. It reached Neptune (right) three years later, in 1989.

    Voyager 2 flew by Uranus and Neptune, too. Then both probes flew farther. In 2012, *Voyager 1* left the solar system. In 2018, *Voyager 2* left. The probes continued to send data.

THE GOLDEN RECORD
Each Voyager probe carried a record. These disks had images and sounds from Earth. The covers explained how to play them. If aliens found the records, they could learn about Earth.

CHAPTER 4

More Missions

Many scientists worked on orbiting probes. One probe reached Jupiter in 1995. Another reached Saturn in 2004. These probes orbited for years.

Workers build the *Cassini-Huygens* probe in 1997. The probe orbited Saturn from 2004 to 2017.

FAST FACT
Juno had a public camera. Regular people could help choose what *Juno* took pictures of.

The *Juno* probe launched in 2011. In 2016, it reached Jupiter. It started orbiting. The probe studied the planet's atmosphere.

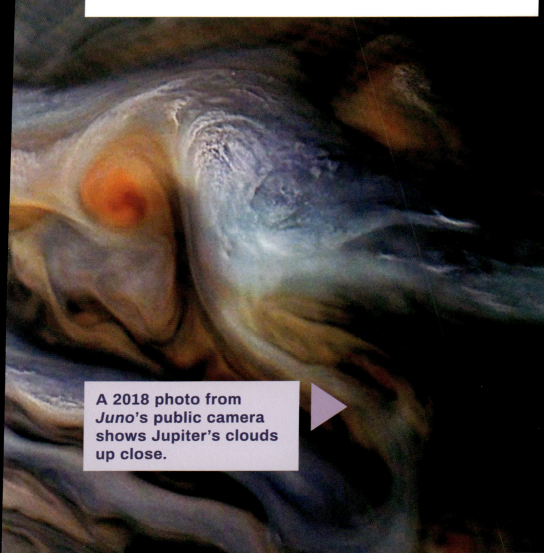

A 2018 photo from *Juno*'s public camera shows Jupiter's clouds up close.

Scientists also wanted to learn more about the Sun. One probe launched in 2018. Another entered space in 2020. They flew closer than ever to the Sun.

In March 2022, the *Solar Orbiter* was halfway between Earth and the Sun.

HOT AS THE SUN

The *Parker Solar Probe* flies close to the Sun. The front of the craft gets very hot. So, the probe has a thick shield.

The *Parker Solar Probe*'s heat shield is 4.5 inches (11.4 cm) thick.

COMPREHENSION QUESTIONS

Write your answers on a separate piece of paper.

1. Write a few sentences that explain the main ideas of Chapter 2.

2. If you could send a probe into space, where would you send it? Why?

3. How long did it take *New Horizons* to reach Pluto?
    - A. less than a year
    - B. more than nine years
    - C. more than 20 years

4. Why might scientists use probes instead of spacecraft with people?
    - A. It is hard to take care of astronauts on long missions.
    - B. Astronauts cannot take photographs.
    - C. Probes do not need fuel.

5. What does **competition** mean in this book?

*This **competition** was between the United States and the Soviet Union. They tried to explore parts of space first.*

    A. a type of country
    B. a spacecraft that can orbit objects
    C. an event where groups try to beat one another

6. What does **public** mean in this book?

*Juno had a **public** camera. Regular people could help choose what Juno took pictures of.*

    A. able to be used by only scientists
    B. not able to be used
    C. able to be used by all people

Answer key on page 32.

GLOSSARY

data
Information collected to study or track something.

dwarf planet
A ball-shaped object that orbits the Sun but is smaller than a planet.

gravity
A force that pulls objects toward planets, stars, and other objects.

orbited
Followed a curved path around an object in space.

probe
A type of spacecraft that gathers information.

radio signals
Waves that can send sound or other information.

solar system
An area that includes the Sun and all of the planets and other objects that move around it.

Soviet Union
A country in Europe and Asia that existed from 1922 to 1991.

TO LEARN MORE

BOOKS

Goldstein, Margaret J. *Mysteries of Deep Space*. Minneapolis: Lerner Publications, 2021.

Morey, Allan. *Exploring Space.* Minneapolis: Bellwether Media, 2023.

Stratton, Connor. *Space Exploration*. Mendota Heights, MN: Focus Readers, 2023.

ONLINE RESOURCES

Visit **www.apexeditions.com** to find links and resources related to this title.

ABOUT THE AUTHOR

Dalton Rains is an author and editor from Saint Paul, Minnesota. He loves to learn about new science discoveries.

D
data, 8–9, 20

J
Juno, 24–25
Jupiter, 6, 18–19, 22, 25

M
Mariner probes, 14–15
Mars, 15
Moon, 14

N
Neptune, 20
New Horizons, 4, 6, 8–9

O
orbiting, 12, 22, 25

P
Parker Solar Probe, 27
pictures, 8, 15, 24
Pluto, 4, 6, 8

S
Saturn, 18, 22
Space Race, 13
Sputnik 1, 12
Sun, 26–27

U
Uranus, 20

V
Venus, 14
Voyager probes, 18–21

ANSWER KEY:
1. Answers will vary; 2. Answers will vary; 3. B; 4. A; 5. C; 6. C